NATO: Does it Still Fulfil an Important Function?

SAGHIR IQBAL

ISBN-10: 1725092816
ISBN-13: 978-1725092815

DEDICATION

I dedicate this book to all those who gave me encouragement, support and guidance. Foremost, to my father (late) Raja Mohammed Iqbal and to my mother Azra Begum, from whom I have learnt so much.

CONTENTS

ACKNOWLEDGMENTS

I am very grateful to a host of people for their various contributions towards this book. I am particularly very grateful to Professor Syed Peerzada Mahmud Shah Bookhari who deserves much commendation for his constant encouragement and support throughout the hard times of the programme.

NATO: Does it Still Fulfil an Important Function?

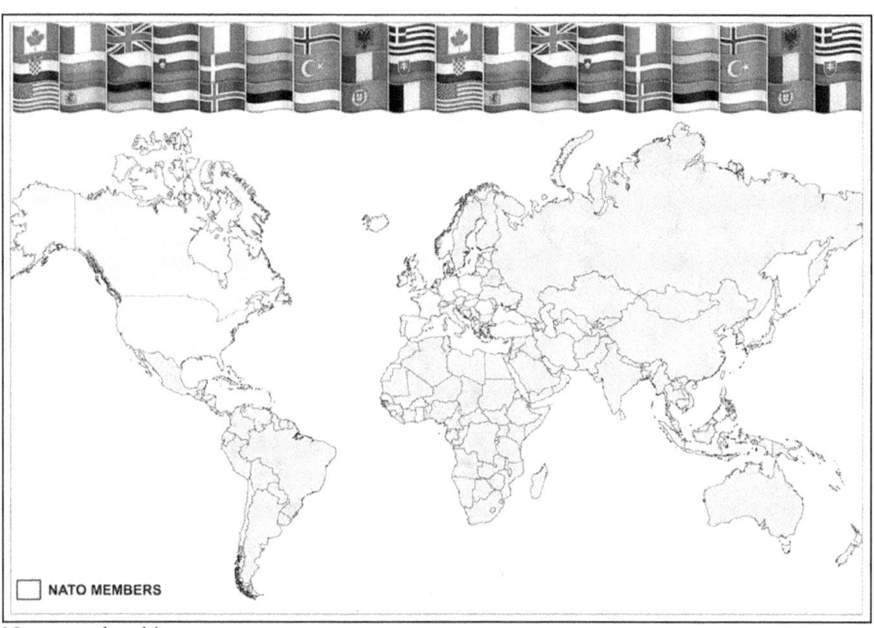

Nato membership map

Abstract

When NATO was founded in 1949, it had a clearly defined role. However, the global security challenges after the post-Cold war period has affected many countries. The demise of the USSR and subsequently the Warsaw Pact resulted in questioning whether NATO should also be disbanded. The reason for NATO was essentially a military alliance to deter Soviet and Warsaw Pact aggression – however, once the threat had finished its role had been challenged by many academics and governments.

In view of the situations, NATO has managed to address new issues and adapt its roles on different levels. It has conducted many operations in crisis regions within Europe and other regions, such as Afghanistan (ISAF forces). With a resurgent Russia and the crisis in Ukraine, the Middle East and Afghanistan – It is argued by some scholars that its role is vital to maintain stability and a deterrence to any would be aggressors.

NATO military exercise

Abbreviation

AWACS – Airborne Warning and Control System

ESDI - European Security and Defence Identity

EU - European Union

ESDP - European Security and Defence Policy

ISAF – International Security Assistance Force

KFOR - Kosovo Force

MBT – Main Battle Tank

NATO – North Atlantic Treaty Organisation

NACC - North Atlantic Cooperation Council

PfP - Partnership for Peace

PGM - Precision guided munitions (Smart weapons)

SAM – Surface to Air Missile

UN – United Nations

UK – United Kingdom

USA – United States of America

WMD - Weapons of Mass Destruction

MBT in action

NATO troops

1 NATO: INTRODUCTION

When NATO was founded in 1949, it had a clearly defined role. It was an alliance for collective security against the Soviet Union and the Warsaw Pact, whereby if one member state was attacked; the rest would come to her aid under article 5. The end of the Cold War left a huge question mark over an alliance designed, in the words of its first Secretary-General Lord Ismay, **to 'keep the Russians out, the Americans in and the Germans down'.**[1] In the immediate post-Cold War years, NATO was seen as serving three purposes: providing an 'insurance policy' against future resurgent Russia; acting as the Primary forum for transatlantic relations; and serving a multilateral constraint on a reunified Germany.[2]

Russian military might on display

---

[1] Jennifer Medcalf, NATO, Oneworld Publications, 2006, p3.
[2] Adrian Hyde-Price, European security in the Twenty-first Century, Routledge Publishers, 2007, p78.

With the declaration of the ending of the Cold War in 1990 and the dissolution of the Soviet Union in 1991, there arose some disputes among scholars over the issue of whether the organization will survive or not in the absence of a Soviet threat. There were concerns of whether the futures of Europe and the United States were bound together as they were during the Cold War, and many European countries seemed to pursue radically different, more pacifistic foreign policies to that of America.[3]

NATO firepower - F-16 Combat aircraft

Many analysts felt that NATO was nothing more than an out of date alliance from the Cold War with no real future. Others would say, however, that an organisation such as NATO was still crucial in the modern world to ensure that countries do not act unilaterally, but co-operate with allies.[4]

---

[3] Op cit:86
[4] Ibid

Typhoon combat aircraft

Russian armoured forces military exercise

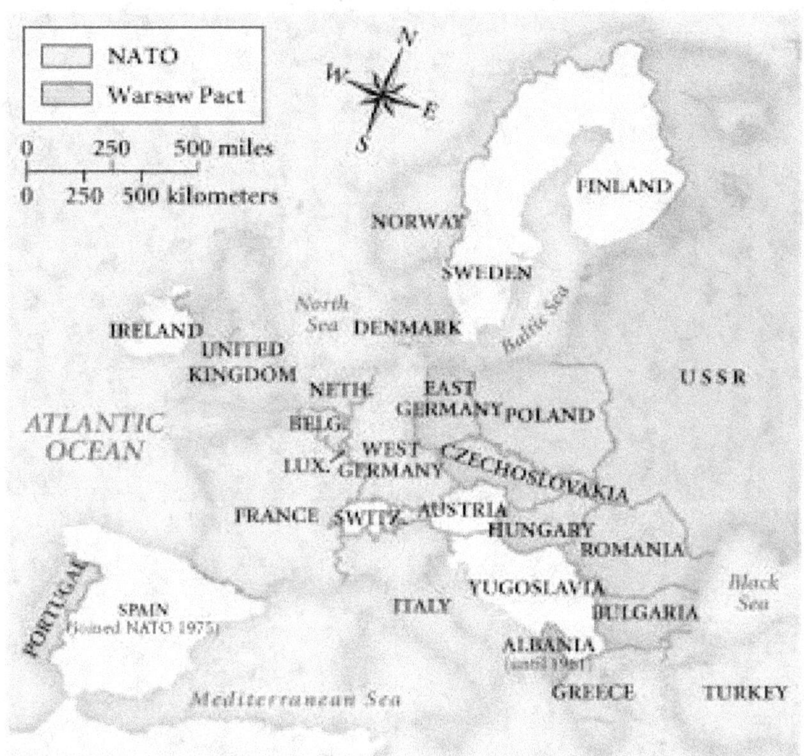

NATO – WARSAW Map[5]

https://twitter.com/historyfacts247/status/837914260948807680

---

[5] http://mapandcounters.blogspot.com/2009/12/spi-nato-1973.html

Russian Bear long range strategic bomber being escorted by an RAF Typhoon fighter jet

Russian frogfoot attack aircraft

Russian military drills involving 12,700 troops, 70 aircraft, 250 tanks and 10 battleships testing their firepower against an imaginary foe close to borders with Poland and the Baltic States.[6]

Russian su-35 combat aircraft

---

[6] Russia launches war games on NATO's eastern flank -
https://www.financialexpress.com/world-news/russia-launches-war-games-on-natos-eastern-flank/855291/

There are currently 29 countries from Europe and North America, that are part of NATO. They liaise and cooperate in the defence and security related areas.[7] A number of operations have been conducted to ensure peace in the region and also acting as a deterrent to any would be aggressor. NATO has participated in a variety of missions, these range from peacekeeping and combat operations, large-scale exercises, training programmes, air defence activities, patrol and reconnaissance missions, as well as disaster response.[8]

In 1994, NATO was involved in its first major combat operation in Bosnia Herzegovina in the former Yugoslavian nation.[9]

NATO headquarters in Brussels Belgium[10]

We will look at a brief background of what NATO is and the role it has undertaken. We will look at its transformation during the demise of the cold war period. The new challenges faced by NATO and how it has adapted to

---

[7] NATO - https://www.nato.int/nato-on-the-map/#lat=53.7881984&lon=-1.7680680999999367&zoom=0&layer-1

[8] Ibid

[9] NATO - https://www.nato.int/nato-on-the-map/#lat=53.7881984&lon=-1.7680680999999367&zoom=0&layer-1

[10] NATO: Seeking Relevance in the 21st Century - https://www.huffingtonpost.com/joseph-v-micallef/nato-seeking-relevance-in_b_13988636.html

the new environment and finally conclude by indicating the important function it continues to perform.

Mechanised forces

NATO's Sophisticated air power

2 BACKGROUND - NORTH ATLANTIC TREATY ORGANIZATION (NATO)

Background - North Atlantic Treaty Organization (NATO)

NATO has been and still is one of the most successful and effective alliance of its kind. For over 69 years NATO has played an important role in protecting the security and freedom of its member countries and in maintaining peace. Although NATO functions primarily as a military alliance, it has played a large role politically. Article 5 of the treaty still stands as the primary mission statement of NATO: **that an attack on one or more NATO members will be considered an attack on all**, in defence of which all other members will collectively take appropriate action, including the use of armed force.[11]

It was originally created to take a stand against the growing strength of the communist Soviet Union after the end of World War II. The treaty formed an allied relationship between the United States, Canada, and Western Europe. If the Soviet Union attacked any of them they would all come together to retaliate collectively. At the end of the war Europe was weak politically and devastated economically. The new enemy was the threat of Communist expansion, but together rather than individually these allies

---

[11] NATO/OTAN - Handbook, NATO's Public Diplomacy Division, 2006, p372.

could take a stand more effectively.[12]

NATO was established on April 4, 1949, when the North Atlantic Treaty Organisation was signed in Washington DC. The initial members are the USA, France, UK, Belgium, Canada, Denmark, Iceland, Luxembourg, Italy, Netherlands, Norway and Portugal.[13]

US President Harry Truman signing the treaty creating NATO[14]

Currently NATO consists of 29 members, they are the following:

Albania, Belgium, Bulgaria, Canada, Croatia, Czech Republic, Denmark, Estonia, France, Germany, Greece, Hungary, Iceland, Italy, Latvia, Lithuania, Luxembourg, Montenegro, Netherlands, Norway, Poland, Portugal, Romania, Slovakia, Slovenia, Spain, Turkey, United Kingdom,

---

[12] (6) Ibid

[13] NATO - https://www.nato.int/cps/en/natohq/who_is_who.htm

[14] NATO: Seeking Relevance in the 21st Century -
https://www.huffingtonpost.com/joseph-v-micallef/nato-seeking-relevance-in_b_13988636.html

United States.[15]

In contrast to the formation of NATO, the Soviet Union had created the Warsaw Pact – an alliance of communist countries it controlled in Eastern Europe.

After the collapse of the Soviet Union and the reunification of Germany, the Warsaw Pact ended in the early 1990s, NATO's original mission was now complete. Since then, NATO has been redefining itself according to its new missions and goals. There have been six main changes which NATO has adapted, in order to address the new security concerns and also to confirm its new role by sending the message to the cynics that NATO is still vital and has a role in the 'new' era.

---

[15] Ibid

NATO's quick response to a potential incident

NATO/Warsaw Pact members

Amphibious warfare

Warsaw Pact tactics

NATO relies on sophisticated air power to counter the numerical forces of the Russians.

Russian troops on parade

Russian troops on parade

NATO Firepower

3 NATO'S POST-COLD WAR ADAPTATION

We will now look briefly at the six major changes which NATO has adapted:

(1) - to perform non-article 5 crisis Management (peace-making/peacekeeping)

First change is mainly a functional. It has enabled NATO to perform non-article 5 crisis management, peace-making and peace keeping operations, initially under the authority of the UN but eventually as a self-authorising force.

NATO forces in action

NATO's new crisis-management and peace support roles took on increasing importance from the mid-1990s. Between 1992 and 1995, NATO forces became involved in the Bosnian war in support of the United Nations, helping monitor and enforce UN sanctions in the Adriatic as well as the no-fly zone over Bosnia and Herzegovina and providing close air support to the UN Protection Force on the ground. Air strikes, launched in August and September 1995 to lift the siege of Sarajevo, helped shift the balance of power and secure a peace settlement. NATO subsequently deployed a UN-mandated, multinational force to implement the military aspects of the peace agreement, in December 1995.[16]

In the spring of 1999, NATO's crisis management role was reinforced when the Allies launched an air operation against the Yugoslav regime to force it to comply with international demands to end political and ethnic repression in the province of Kosovo. A large NATO-led multinational force was then sent in to help restore stability.[17]

NATO's airpower

---

[16] Official NATO Website - http://www.nato.int/home.htm
[17] Ibid

NATO's warship on sea exercises

In early 2001, NATO, in cooperation with the new democratic Yugoslav government, engaged in crisis prevention in Southern Serbia, an area with a large ethnic Albanian population. Later in the same year, NATO together with the European Union engaged in preventive diplomacy to help avoid the outbreak of civil war in the Former Yugoslav Republic of Macedonia, by encouraging negotiations on a peace plan. A small NATO force deployed in the summer to peacefully disarm the rebels and provide security for international observers, and stability was soon restored.[18]

The Balkan operations have allowed NATO forces to build up a great deal of experience in peace-support and crisis-management operations, and in leading multinational coalitions also involving non-NATO countries. Thereafter, since the early 1990s NATO has been involved in a number of operations and missions,[19] such as the following:

- Approximately 20,000 troops are involved in NATO missions around the world.
- NATO is currently operating in Afghanistan, Kosovo and the

---

[18] Ibid

[19] Operations and Missions - https://www.nato.int/cps/en/natohq/topics_52060.htm?

Mediterranean.

- NATO is also supporting the African Union and directing air policing missions on the invitation of its Allies.
- The European response to the refugee and migrant crisis is being tackled by NATO.
- In Turkey, NATO has deployed sophisticated Patriot missiles and AWACS aircraft.
- NATO also carries out disaster relief operations and missions to protect populations against natural, technological or humanitarian disasters.[20]

NATO mobility – power projection capability

NATO has shown that if peace and security fails around the world – it has the necessary military might to deal with any crisis management operations. It has demonstrated its ability to deal with any crisis on an individual basis or by co-operating with other nations. It is for this reason that many other nations see NATO as a deterrent to any would be aggressor.

---

[20] Operations and Missions - https://www.nato.int/cps/en/natohq/topics_52060.htm?

NATO/UN Forces in Bosnia

(2) - Geographic – NATO's role in global security whilst retaining a defensive role.

Second change is geographic, illustrated by the non-article 5 missions outside the territory of NATO's members (as defined by article 6 of the Washington Treaty). This functional and geographic change therefore illustrates how NATO has made the transition from being a defensive alliance focused on Western Europe, to one that contributes to global security whilst retaining a defensive role.[21]

http://www.oroszvilag.hu/?t1=posztszovjet_terseg_hirei&hid=1305

---

[21] Jennifer Medcalf, NATO, Oneworld Publications, 2006, p52.

For Instance, in Afghanistan, the Alliance agreed in August 2003 to take on command of the International Security Assistance Force (ISAF) to help bring stability to the country and eradicate any areas for 'terrorists' to operate (safe haven). The enhanced NATO role ensures continuity and overcomes the problem of having to find new nations to lead the mission every six months. NATO personnel operate under the ISAF banner and continue to work within a UN mandate, which was expanded in October 2003 to allow for operations beyond the capital, Kabul.[22]

NATO's engagement in Afghanistan is the Alliance's first mission beyond the Euro-Atlantic area. Following the US-led intervention against Saddam Hussein's regime, NATO has agreed to support the Polish-led multinational division in central Iraq with force generation, logistics, communications and intelligence. It is prepared to offer similar support to other Allies that request it.[23]

The post-September 11 security environment has also seen the classic use of sea power against new threats. Since October 2001, under Operation Active Endeavour, NATO ships have been patrolling the Eastern Mediterranean, monitoring shipping to detect and deter terrorist activity. The mission has since been extended to include escorting non-military shipping, upon request, through the Straits of Gibraltar, as well as to include the systematic boarding of suspect ships.[24]

ISAF Forces

---

[22] (11)Official NATO Website - http://www.nato.int/home.htm
[23] (12)Ibid
[24] (12)Ibid

Operation Active Endeavour

(3) - Internal adaptation – ESDI type role

Third change concerns internal adaptation which can be demonstrated by the emergence and consolidation of the European 'pillar' through the European Security and Defence Identity (ESDI).[25] This was a measure that was designed to increase the role and capabilities of the European NATO Allies. Since the ESDI programme was introduced in the mid-1990s, NATO has also initiated and concluded a set of agreements with the European Union (EU) in order to facilitate co-operation between NATO and the EU's European Security and Defence Policy (ESDP).[26]

Additionally, NATO has supported the strengthening of a European defence pillar via EU and endorsed the concept of Combined Joint Task Force; (separable but not separate military capabilities).[27]

---

[25] https://www.nato.int/docu/topics/eng/page04.pdf

[26] Jennifer Medcalf, NATO, Oneworld Publications, 2006, p84.

[27] Ibid

NATO MBT on manoeuvres

(4) - NATO Outreach Programmes

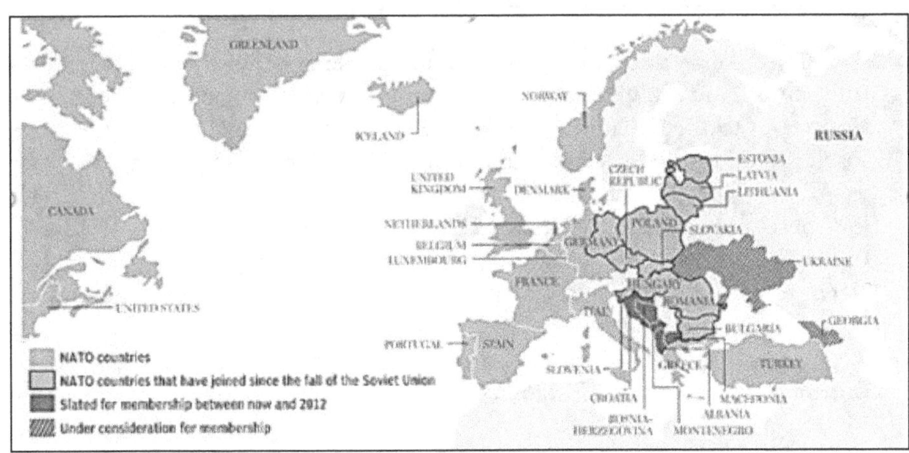

Fourth change is the emergence and consolidation of outreach programmes
to NATO's former Warsaw Pact adversaries, through North Atlantic

Cooperation Council (NACC), Partnership for Peace (PfP) programmes, Mediterranean Dialogue, Special Partnership agreements with Russia and Ukraine.

The expansion of NATO has been an important issue. As well as admitting new full members into the organization, NATO has reached out to 26 non-member countries to take part in its Partnership for Peace program. The Alliance adapted to the post-Cold War strategic context by adopting a broader definition of security and launching a broad-based strategy of partnership and cooperation throughout the Euro-Atlantic area, which is now regarded as one of NATO's fundamental security tasks. The process was initiated in 1990, when Allied leaders extended a hand of friendship across the former East-West divide, proposing a new cooperative relationship with countries of Central and Eastern Europe and former Soviet republics.[28]

This set the scene for the creation of the North Atlantic Cooperation Council (NACC) in December 1991, as a forum for consultation aimed at building mutual trust. A few years later, the partnership process took a significant leap forward with the launch, in 1994, of the Partnership for Peace (PfP) - a major programme of practical bilateral cooperation between NATO and individual Partners. The purpose of the Partnership for Peace is to increase stability, diminish threats to peace and build strengthened security relationships between individual Partner countries and NATO as well as with other Partner countries.[29]

Dialogue with Mediterranean countries

Several of NATO's southern European members border the Mediterranean and security and stability in the Mediterranean area are therefore of major importance to the Alliance. Indeed, the security of the whole of Europe is closely linked to security and stability in the Mediterranean region.

For these reasons, in 1995, NATO launched a new dialogue with six countries in the southern part of the Mediterranean region, namely Egypt, Israel, Jordan, Mauritania, Morocco and Tunisia. Algeria became a participant in February 2000. The Mediterranean Dialogue, which is an integral part of the Alliance's cooperative approach to security, aims to contribute to security and stability in the region, to achieve better mutual

---

[28] Charles Krupnick, Almost NATO – partners and Players in Central and Eastern European Security, Rowman & Littlefield Publishers, 2003, p22.
[29] Ibid

understanding and to correct misperceptions about NATO in Dialogue countries.[30]

New ties with Russia

NATO has been building bridges and developing cooperation with Russia since the early 1990s. The rationale for cooperation between NATO countries and Russia is clear: common security challenges are best tackled through cooperation and Russia's involvement is critical for any comprehensive post-Cold War European security system.

In the wake of the September 2001 terrorist attacks, which reinforced the need for coordinated action to respond to common threats, the NATO-Russia partnership was given new impetus and substance at the Rome Summit in May 2002. A new NATO-Russia Council (NRC) was created, which brings together the NATO Allies and Russia as equal partners to identify and pursue opportunities for joint action. Cooperation is being intensified in key areas of mutual interest and concern.[31]

Partnership with Ukraine

NATO's relationship with Ukraine recognises the importance of an independent, stable and democratic Ukraine and the country's declared intention to increase its integration in European and Euro-Atlantic structures. This was expressed in the 1997 Charter on a Distinctive Partnership, which provides the formal basis for consultations with NATO on Euro-Atlantic security issues and established the NATO-Ukraine Commission (NUC) to direct cooperative activities.[32]

NATO-Ukraine relations date back to 1991, when Ukraine joined the North Atlantic Cooperation Council, immediately upon achieving independence with the break-up of the Soviet Union. The country's aspirations towards Euro-Atlantic integration were also later reflected in 1994, when it became the first of the Commonwealth of Independent States to join the Partnership for Peace. Ukraine's commitment to contribute to Euro-Atlantic security has since been demonstrated in its support for NATO and its Allies in peacekeeping and crisis management

---

[30] W.Park & G.Wyn Rees, Rethinking security in Post-Cold war Europe, Addison Wesley Longman Limited, 1998, p143.
[31] Ronald D. Asmus, Opening NATO's Door – How the Alliance remade itself for a new era, Columbia University Press, 2002, p191.
[32] NATO/OTAN - Handbook, NATO's Public Diplomacy Division, 2006, p219.

operations.[33]

(5) - Enlargement of NATO's membership

Fifth change was the enlargement of NATO's membership. NATO membership is open to any European country. Article 10 of the Washington Treaty allows existing members to invite 'any European State in a position to further the principles of this Treaty and to contribute to the security of the North Atlantic area' to become a member. NATO's 12 founding members have grown to 29 today after five rounds of enlargement. NATO's door remains open for new members.[34]

The aim of each round of enlargement has been to extend Euro-Atlantic security and to increase NATO's strength, cohesion and vitality, and has not been directed against the security interests of any third country. Each round of enlargement has helped extend security and stability in Europe and heal the wounds of a continent, which suffered two wars in the first half of the 20th century and was then divided by an Iron Curtain for forty years. Many former Warsaw Pact adversaries are now NATO members

---

[33] Ibid

[34] Sean Kay, NATO and the Future of European Security, Rowman & Littlefield Publishers, 1998, p89.

with other's also applying.[35]

NATO's maritime security

(6) - New Threats

Sixth change was NATO's response to the 'new' threats of international terrorism and the proliferation of weapons of mass destruction (WMD) after Sept 11 2001 attacks on America. For the first time in NATO's history, article 5 was invoked. As mentioned earlier, Article 5 is the core clause of the Washington Treaty, NATO's founding charter, which states that an armed attack against one Ally shall be considered an attack against them all.[36]

In response to an invocation of Article 5, each Ally determines, in consultation with other Allies, how it can best contribute to any action deemed necessary to restore and maintain the security of the North Atlantic area, including the use of armed force. Article 5 was first invoked on 12 September 2001 immediately following the 11 September terrorist attacks against the United States. The invocation was initially provisional, pending determination that the attacks were directed from abroad. This was

---

[35] Op cit:91
[36] Lawrence S.Kaplan, NATO Divided/NATO United – The evolution of an Alliance, Praeger Publishers, 2004, p134.

confirmed on 2 October 2001, after US officials presented findings on investigations into the attacks to the North Atlantic Council, concluding that the al-Qaida terrorist network was responsible.[37]

AWACS aircraft on NATO ISAF operations

On 4 October, the Allies agreed a series of measures to assist the US-led campaign against terrorism. These include enhanced intelligence sharing and cooperation, blanket over-flight clearances and access to ports and airfields for US and other Allied craft for operations against terrorism, and the deployment of part of NATO's standing naval forces to the Eastern Mediterranean and of the Alliance's airborne warning and control systems (AWACS) aircraft to the United States.[38]

Overall, as the strategic environment changes, NATO will likely have to evolve increasingly rapidly to meet new threats to its member states. However, the basic tenets of cooperation within the Alliance, namely shared values and interests, remain true to the principles of its founding treaty.

---

[37] Op cit:135
[38] Ibid

NATO firepower – US Aircraft carriers

4 CONTINENTAL DRIFT?

Ever since the end of the Cold War NATO has been spreading its wings even further and has become involved in a whole range of missions in relation not only to defence but also greatly to peacekeeping. After the attacks of September 11th the focus of NATO shifted mostly to counteracting terrorism. The decision to do so was unanimous as it was an issue that all parties felt worthy of retaliating to. There was no discrepancy in the decision.

However, such consistency was not displayed when the decision was being made about sending NATO troops to engage in activities in Iraq. Consensus was not reached with either NATO or the United Nations. The Balkans tragedy suggests flexibility and a multi-faceted approach to security are needed in the future. The Bosnian conflict was sparked by a desire for independence. Serbia was fast losing its dominance over the other Yugoslav republics, had already lost Slovenia and wanted to regain control. In doing so a four-year conflict followed killing 278,000 at a rough estimate, while Europe and the west seemed lethargic to respond.[39]

On a basic level it showed the USA was needed to sort things out. After all, Luxembourg Foreign Minister, Jacques Poos had declared as early as 1991, "if one problem can be solved by the Europeans, it's the Yugoslav problem.

---

[39] Adrian Hyde-Price, European security in the Twenty-first Century, Routledge Publishers, 2007, p92.

This is a European problem and it's not up to the Americans and not up to anyone else."[40] The Europeans failed. Equally Bosnia suggests the UN was unprepared to deal with military crisis, never mind ethnic cleansing. It has been argued, with justification the UN in Bosnia made things worse, showed itself to be practically inept and set confidence in the UN's ability back decades.

In 1999 the Balkans again caused European security difficulties. Kosovo erupted as Serbia sought to control the last remnants of Yugoslavia. The Kosovo Liberation Army sought independence for the Albanian majority and civil unrest followed. The Serb's brutal crackdown forced Europe and the west to act; NATO commenced a bombing campaign that forced Serbia to retreat in weeks.[41]

Meanwhile in the former Warsaw Pact, changes were occurring as each nation undertook the long and arduous journey to democracy. As Ian Clark states, 'The European armistice had been struck: the full settlement was still impending.' They may have been freed from the 'Motherland,' but were left economically impoverished as their previous dependence was gone. It is testament both to the leaders in those countries and the wider community for making sure east Europe did not go the 'Balkan way.' This was more relevant for the west as these nations were on their doorsteps.[42]

Trans-national institutions were not covered in glory during the 1990's, but what experience tells us, is they will be more important in future security matters. NATO may not be perfect, but it did bring about the end of the Kosovo crisis. Equally its increased membership and commitment to a new rapid reaction force means it will have 40,000 troops ready to maintain security.[43]

Finally the experience of the 1990's would seem to suggest the future of European Security may well be in the hands of the Americans. Richard Holbrook said in Bosnia, "this was the most important test of American leadership since the end of the cold war." They arguably sorted out the Balkan problems with the Dayton Accords and Kosovo bombing, of which they carried out 90% of sorties. The 1990's showed the Americans that the

---

[40] Ibid

[41] NATO/OTAN – The Prague Summit and NATO's Transformation, A readers guide, NATO 2003, p62.

[42] Ibid

[43] Adrian Hyde-Price, European security in the Twenty-first Century, Routledge Publishers, 2007, p92.

dependant relationship they had fostered during the cold war could not just be terminated. Indeed it is clear the Americans have sought to make this dependence more prevalent by placing themselves ever more firmly in NATO and in calling for a global coalition against terror. As long as they seek European support and the Europeans are happy to get protection and global security on the cheap, this should continue.[44]

MBT formations

US Aircraft carriers gives NATO an edge in operations

---

[44] Ibid

NATO Military exercise

US B1B- Bomber NATO exercise

5 CONCLUSION

The demise of the Cold War, the disintegration of the Soviet Union and the collapse of communism in the period from 1989 to 1991 called into question NATO's future role and its continued existence. The primary role was called into question over its future relevance in the post-Cold War world. The realization that the Cold War status quo was not sustainable in the post-Cold War context therefore provided the impetus for the Allies to reform NATO, the results of which can be seen in the process of adaptation that NATO has undergone since the early 1990s (the six changes mentioned earlier).

Stephen E. Meyers commented in 2003 on the questions about NATO's vitality:

NATO's time has come and gone, and today there is no legitimate reason for it to exist. Although the strong differences exhibited in the Alliance over the war against Iraq have accelerated NATO's irrelevancy, the root cause of its problems go much deeper. Consequently, for both the United States and Europe, NATO is at best an irrelevant distraction and at worst toxic to their respective contemporary security needs.[45]

However, since the 9/11 incident, it indicates that, rather than there being no legitimate reason for it to exist, it still continues to address the

---

[45] Jennifer Medcalf, NATO, Oneworld Publications, 2006, p180.

contemporary security needs of the Allies. It can be argued that NATO is the world's most effective permanent coalition and is very capable of coordinating military action. An integrated military alliance pools the capabilities of its member states for mutual benefit. In response to the current 'War on Terrorism', NATO has not played a very large direct role in the current conflict, but NATO has provided the framework that allowed the United States to call on those countries that are involved in the war. This is because NATO allies share joint-force planning and training, integrated and interoperable military forces and habits of cooperation that have been developed through decades of working together.

NATO allies sent troops to Afghanistan, invoked Article 5 of its treaty declaring that the attack on America was an attack on all. Furthermore, NATO has played a vital role in stabilizing the Balkans. It was NATO intervention that ended the conflict in Bosnia, and NATO action in Kosovo that defeated Slobodan Milosevic's ethnic cleansing and eventually led to his downfall. It was NATO and European diplomacy that prevented ethnic conflict in Macedonia from erupting into a crisis that would have distracted attention away from the war on terrorism.[46]

More broadly, the enlargement of NATO to include new members from Eastern and Central Europe has served as a magnet for the emergence of democratic governments in the region that was a central ideological

---

[46] Christoph Bertram, Europe in the Balance, Carnegie Endowment for international Peace, 1995, p19.

battlefield of the Cold War.

Although the world has changed substantially since NATO was first convened, NATO retains a vital role in helping to manage relations with Russia and former members of the Soviet Union and in helping control crises throughout Europe. Equally important, it helps to enhance the development of new democracies and ultimately is critical to the international cooperation needed to combat terrorism.

Certainly, only remnants are left of the roles that NATO played during the Cold War. As mentioned earlier, Lord Ismay stated that NATO's role was to 'keep the Russians out, the Americans in and the Germans down'.[47] While this is no longer the case, managing relations with Russia, providing a framework for German defense and linking the United States to Europe remain important roles to this day.

Russian soldiers on parade

While challenges of terrorism and weapons of mass destruction often arise outside NATO's immediate area, and the organization may not be involved as such, it makes an important difference that allied militaries have trained in the frequent NATO exercises. It means that NATO countries can operate effectively together even when not all members of the organization are officially involved.

Finally, new threats are posed by the war on terrorism that cannot be met

---

[47] Jennifer Medcalf, NATO, Oneworld Publications, 2006, p3.

solely by military means. More will need to be done in coordinating intelligence, preparing defenses against cyber-attacks and sharing best practices in making homeland security more robust in NATO member nations. NATO exists as an effective framework for coordinating preparations in the security area.

None of this is to deny that NATO faces some problems. Since the end of the cold war in the 1990s, many predicted that NATO would become obsolete with the end of the Cold War. A resurgent Russia and its threat to Ukraine and Georgia has highlighted the need for a strong collective organisation – it can be argued that the current crisis in Europe/Russia and other simmering disputes across the globe have justified the existence of NATO. On the contrary, it remains popular in national capitals and, despite the cynics is relevant to the new challenges.

NATO soldiers

AWACS aircraft

US F-15 Eagle combat aircraft

Nato forces

Russian MBT on parade

References

Adrian Hyde-Price. (2007). European security in the Twenty-first Century, Routledge Publishers.

Charles Krupnick. (2003). Almost NATO – partners and Players in Central and Eastern European Security, Rowman & Littlefield Publishers.

Christoph Bertram. (1995). Europe in the Balance, Carnegie Endowment for international Peace.

Jennifer Medcalf. (2006). NATO, Oneworld Publications.

Lawrence S.Kaplan. (2004) NATO Divided/NATO United – The evolution of an Alliance, Praeger Publishers.

NATO: Seeking Relevance in the 21st Century - https://www.huffingtonpost.com/joseph-v-micallef/nato-seeking-relevance-in_b_13988636.html

NATO/OTAN (2003). The Prague Summit and NATO's Transformation, A readers guide.

NATO/OTAN (2006) - Handbook, NATO's Public Diplomacy Division.

Official NATO Website - http://www.nato.int/home.htm

NATO - https://www.nato.int/nato-on-the-map/#lat=53.7881984&lon=-1.7680680999999367&zoom=0&layer-1

Ronald D. Asmus. (2002). Opening NATO's Door – How the Alliance remade itself for a new era, Columbia University Press.

Sean Kay. (1998). NATO and the Future of European Security, Rowman & Littlefield Publishers.

Ted Galen Carpenter. (2001). NATO Enters the 21st Century, Frank Cass Publishers.

W.Park & G.Wyn Rees. (1998).   Rethinking security in Post-Cold war Europe, Addison Wesley Longman Limited.

Images in this book fall under the following categories

(a) public domain (applicable to most official photos released by the military/maufacturers)

(b) free for commercial use

(c) used with explicit permission from the owner (applicable to all images from private websites)

(d) assumed to fall under (a) or (b) (applicable to images in printed media where no image owner is identified)

Index

Recently released books (2018)

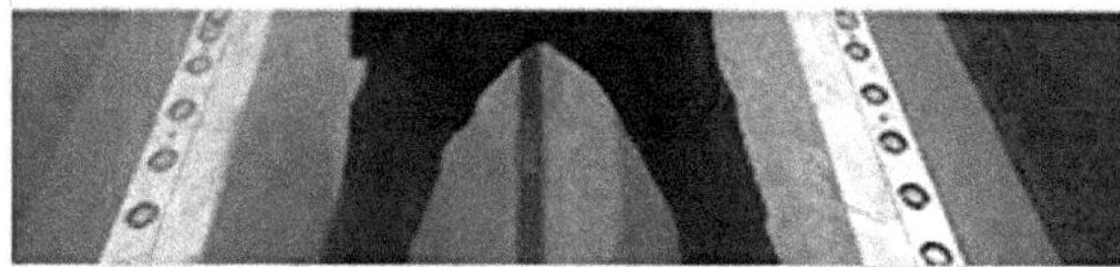

Major changes in East Asia have placed the region near the top of the World's strategic agenda. East Asia has until recently experienced the fastest regional economic growth rate in the world for many years. Economic co-operation has been flourishing and economic interests have become the major reason in reshaping East Asian international relations. However, there have also been changes in the security environment, due to many factors, such as the reduction of US forces in East Asia, the disintegration of the Soviet Union (the decline of the Soviet Union's presence in the region had led to renewed attention to traditional and potential rivalries among the major East Asian powers), and the concern of China's hegemonistic ambitions.

Product details

- **Paperback:** 106 pages
- **Publisher:** CreateSpace Independent Publishing Platform; 1 edition (16 Jan. 2018)
- **Language:** English
- **ISBN-10:** 1974062309
- **ISBN-13:** 978-1974062300
- **Product Dimensions:** 21.6 x 0.6 x 27.9 cm

The astronomical rising costs of modern combat has resulted in many countries being deprived of purchasing a modern combat aircraft and this has had an adverse effect on their security. Many nations have tried to undertake cost-effective measures for their defence needs.

Countries can either purchase very expensive modern aircraft or buy older aircraft that can be expensive to operate due to their high maintenance requirements. The Pakistan Air Force had initiated the plan to co-develop an affordable modern multi-role fighter aircraft with China. Chengdu Aircraft Corporation (CAC) in collaboration with Pakistan Aeronautical Complex (PAC, Kamra) have jointly developed the JF-17 Thunder combat aircraft (also known as the FC-1 Xiaolong Fierce Dragon in China).

JF-17 Thunder is a sophisticated light-weight multi-role, all weather, day/night fighter aircraft that is manufactured by Pakistan and China. The JF-17 Thunder has become a very cost-effective aircraft that costs very little compared to other modern aircraft. Many countries have shown an interest and a few have started to make orders. Some have described the JF-17 as the 'Ultimate MiG-21' arguing that the Chinese/Pakistani JF-17 builds on a classic warplane – although it has no resemblance and its level of sophistication is comparable to current advanced fighter aircraft on the market. This very modern and capable aircraft has the potential to become a potent platform that can serve with numerous air forces across the world. Product details

- **Paperback:** 178 pages
- **Publisher:** CreateSpace Independent Publishing Platform (26 Feb. 2018)
- **Language:** English
- **ISBN-10:** 1984055240
- **ISBN-13:** 978-1984055248
- **Product Dimensions:** 21.6 x 1.1 x 27.9 cm

The global security challenges after the post-Cold war period has affected many countries. Pakistan's geography and location present its security planners with serious, almost irresolvable strategic and tactical problems. It borders the nuclear states of India and China, an ambitious Iran, and an unstable Afghanistan, which is perceived as a gateway to its commercial-strategic ambitions in Central Asia.

Pakistan's key security problems are a reflection of its history and domestic circumstances. The overriding concern of Pakistan is its internal and external security. Strategically, Pakistan lacks territorial depth. Its main cities and communication routes are relatively close to the border with India and are susceptible to attack. In addition, the headwaters of Pakistan's rivers and main irrigation systems originate from India. Pakistan's borders with India were also new and mainly unfortified and, in many places, were drawn in ways that made them indefensible. Because the borders were also un-demarcated, there was abundant chance for conflict. Pakistan has particularly been affected with a number of issues.

It has been argued by many that a Fourth generation/Hybrid war has been imposed on Pakistan, in order to break the nation (Balkanization of Pakistan into different parts) with the aim of making it either extremely weak or total destruction as a nation state (so that it is not able to challenge the hegemonistic ambitions of its adversaries).The purpose of this book is to assess the military security problems that Pakistan faces, and focus on its external security matters (military threats from neighbouring countries such as India, balance of power in the region, nuclear and ballistic missile threats, relationship with external powers, the high risk of war and its role on the 'War on Terror'), and its internal security problems (sectarianism, proliferation of small arms, refugees, ethnic violence, drug problem, economic weaknesses), and also its ability to cope with these problems.
Product details

- **Paperback:** 366 pages
- **Publisher:** CreateSpace Independent Publishing Platform; 1 edition (13 April 2018)
- **Language:** English
- **ISBN-10:** 1986169421
- **ISBN-13:** 978-1986169424
- **Product Dimensions:** 21.6 x 2.2 x 27.9 cm

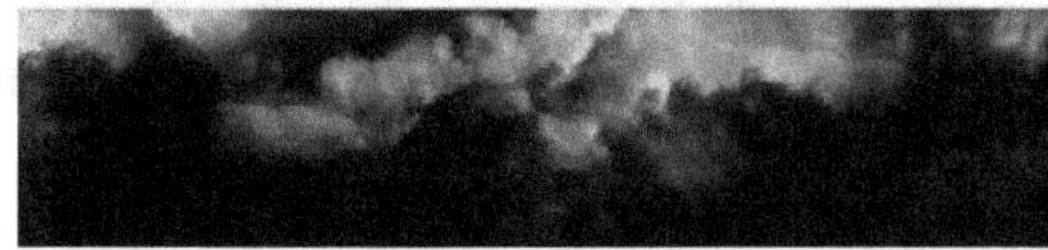

An impending nuclear holocaust is likely to happen, if the world community does not take action. A conflict that has been simmering for many years is beginning to spiral out of control. Two nuclear powers have an unresolved dispute that has increased tensions in the region.

Both countries are purchasing and developing sophisticated state-of-the-art weapons that could unleash great terror and destruction on the populations of both countries – with also serious global ramifications.

The world's most dangerous flashpoint, has the highest chance of a nuclear war occurring – it is deemed by many to be more serious that the Cuban Missile Crisis and North Korea's nuclear sabre rattling. The dispute needs to be amicably resolved between both nations and confidence building measures need to be implemented.

Product details

- **Paperback:** 154 pages
- **Publisher:** CreateSpace Independent Publishing Platform; 1 edition (16 April 2018)
- **Language:** English
- **ISBN-10:** 1717040403
- **ISBN-13:** 978-1717040404
- **Product Dimensions:** 21.6 x 0.9 x 27.9 cm

Pakistan faces a number of threats from internal and external forces – with the aim of weakening the country and an attempt to 'balkanise' Pakistan in to different parts. The Pakistani Chief of Army, General Qamar Javed Bajwa has said that "a hybrid war had been imposed on Pakistan to internally weaken it, but noted that the enemies were failing to divide the country on the basis of ethnicity and other identities".

Furthermore he states, "Our enemies know that they cannot beat us fair and square and have thus subjected us to a cruel, evil and protracted hybrid war. They are trying to weaken our resolve by weakening us from within". Conflicts in Ukraine, Israel and Lebanon (Hizbullah), Syria, Libya, War on Terror in Afghanistan and its impact in Pakistan etc., have resulted in multi-layered efforts to destabilise a functioning state and polarize its society. The centre of gravity is to target population in hybrid warfare. The aim of the adversary is to influence influential policy makers and key decision makers by combining kinetic operations with subversive efforts. The aggressor often resorts to covert actions, to avoid attribution or retribution. At the moment there is no universally accepted definition of hybrid wars – the term is too abstract and is seen by some as using a fancy term to refer to irregular methods to counter conventionally stronger forces.

Accordingly, many say that the new definitions of 4th generation or hybrid wars are really the repackaging of the traditional clash between the armed forces of nation states and the non-state insurgents. This book will be assessing Pakistan's insecurity and the hybrid wars imposed onto it by its adversaries. It will look at a number of issues that Pakistan is facing (military imbalance, economic and political weaknesses, internal and external security threats and the impact of hybrid warfare on Pakistan).

Product details
- **Paperback:** 132 pages
- **Publisher:** CreateSpace Independent Publishing Platform; 1 edition (17 Jun. 2018)
- **Language:** English
- **ISBN-10:** 1721510095
- **ISBN-13:** 978-1721510092

- **Product Dimensions:** 21.6 x 0.8 x 27.9 cm

Each year billions of dollars' worth of arms are procured between various nations, despite the fact that many millions of people live in desperate poverty, many will die from hunger and hunger related diseases. Weapons of increasing firepower and the missiles to deliver them accurately are being acquired, mainly through the Global Arms Trade. This means that we must expect wars in the world to become increasingly violent and destructive.

This book focuses on what the arms trade is and its impact on the world, the wars which have resulted or were sustained by this trade. It is necessary to know which countries sell arms and which ones buy. Also it is important to have some idea of how large the trade is. The international trade in arms has considerably increased since World War 2. Major weapons (aircraft, missiles, tanks and ships) probably account for about one-half of the total trade in weapons and equipment. Many countries and their respective Military-Industrial Complex are 'making a killing' in the world's largest trade in the buying and selling of military technology (weapons).

Product details

- **Paperback:** 90 pages
- **Publisher:** CreateSpace Independent Publishing Platform (28 July 2018)
- **Language:** English
- **ISBN-10:** 1721773150
- **ISBN-13:** 978-1721773152
- **Product Dimensions:** 15.2 x 0.5 x 22.9 cm

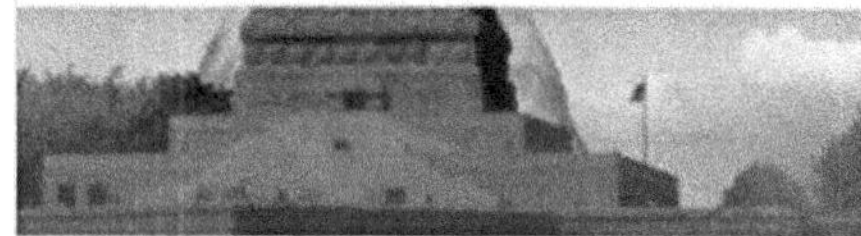

The global security challenges since World War II and thereafter (post-Cold war period) has affected many countries. This has resulted in a number of countries pursuing a nuclear weapons programme to provide them with the ultimate security – the belief that the fear of utter annihilation of their opponents would result in deterrence and eventually detente. According to Kristensen and Norris (2014), there are approximately 16,300 nuclear weapons located at some 97 sites in 14 countries. Many of these weapons are in military arsenals (roughly 10,000), with the remaining ones being in the process of retirement and awaiting dismantlement. Accordingly, 93% of the total global inventory resides in Russia and the United States of America. The remaining weapon stockpiles are in the United Kingdom (UK), France, China, India, Pakistan, North Korea and Israel.

This book looks at the proliferation of weapons of mass destruction (WMD), the double standards and hypocrisy practiced by the five declared nuclear powers. It gives a brief short history of nuclear development in the nuclear countries and the impact of nuclear war. It argues that the only way to eradicate these horrendous weapons is for the five declared nuclear powers to make immediate measures to dismantle the weapons and stockpiles of weaponised materials – as they had agreed under the Nuclear Non-proliferation Treaty (NPT).

Product details

- **Paperback:** 146 pages
- **Publisher:** CreateSpace Independent Publishing Platform (31 July 2018)
- **Language:** English
- **ISBN-10:** 1983910414
- **ISBN-13:** 978-1983910418
- **Product Dimensions:** 15.2 x 0.8 x 22.9 cm

This book looks at the concept of 'terrorism' and its primary aim of creating a climate of fear. Any discussion of terrorism has to firstly define its terms: what do we mean by terrorism and how does it manifest itself in contemporary accounts and moreover, what is the difference between legitimate military action and one based on terror? The definitions of terrorism are complex and depend, to a very large extent, on who one is asking. A government defence adviser would, for instance, have a markedly different notion of what constitutes terrorism than a member of a paramilitary organisation and an ordinary member of the public might have a notion based somewhere on the interaction between these two depending on their socio-cultural background. This is primarily the main reason why the term has not been universally accepted by all scholars or academics.

There are many reasons why political groups attempt to bring about radical change through terrorism. People are often frustrated with their position in society. They may in some way feel persecuted or oppressed because of their race, religion, or they feel exploited by a government. Any group that uses terrorist actions have very complex and powerful reasons to engage in those activities. The usual experience of violence by a stronger party has historically turned victims into terrorists. State terror very often breeds collective terror. Because 'terrorism' is a word that has been used so much and so loosely that it has lost a clear meaning. It can be argued that terrorists are not born, but created as issues of today develop into the conflicts of tomorrow.

Product details

- **Paperback:** 202 pages
- **Publisher:** CreateSpace Independent Publishing Platform (7 Aug. 2018)
- **Language:** English
- **ISBN-10:** 1724714856
- **ISBN-13:** 978-1724714855
- **Product Dimensions:** 15.2 x 1.2 x 22.9 cm

ABOUT THE AUTHOR

Saghir Iqbal is a researcher in International Relations and Security Studies. He is an experienced Intelligence Analyst and has achieved a number of qualifications in this field. He is also a Lecturer in Business Management as well as an Examiner for A Level History and Business. Saghir Iqbal has a subject specialism in the following areas:

International Politics of the Cold War 1945-1991
Conflict Resolution in International Society+
Global and North-South Security Studies
Britain in the World
Disarmament Processes: History and Theory
Nationalism and Ethnicity in Post-Cold War Politics
Middle East: Area in Conflict
European Security
International Politics of the Environment
The United Nations, Peacekeeping and Intervention
Disarmament Processes: Current Problems
Globalisation and the South
International Terrorism
International Politics and Security Studies
Introduction to Peace Studies
Politics of the Global Environment
Regional Security in East Asia
Critical Security studies

Recently released books (2018)

- Dangerous Flashpoints in East Asia: The Military Build-up
- JF-17 Thunder: The Making of a Modern Cost- effective Multi-role Combat Aircraft
- Pakistan's War Machine: An Encyclopedia of its Weapons, Strategy and Military Security
- Miscalculation: Risks of Inadvertent Nuclear War
- Hybrid Warfare and its Impact on Pakistan's Security
- Making a Killing: The Scourge of the Global Arms Trade
- Nuclear Apartheid: Bullying, Hypocrisy and the Double Standards on Nuclear Weapons
- Terrorism: Creating a Climate of Fear

Website: www.saghir.co.uk

www.ingramcontent.com/pod-product-compliance
Lightning Source LLC
Chambersburg PA
CBHW070046260726
48658CB00002B/750